SPEAKING OUT

A Parent's Guide to Recognizing and Responding to the 7 Signs of Child Molestation

DR. MACKLENE. C. JONES

TABLE OF CONTENTS

CHAPTER THREE

CONCLUSION

Introduction

Child sexual abuse is a widespread and painful problem that affects millions of youngsters around the world. According to the World Health Organization, approximately one in every four girls and one in every thirteen males are sexually abused before the age of 18. These figures are concerning, and they emphasize the critical need for parents to be educated and equipped to recognize and respond to indicators of molestation in their children.

The notion of your child being sexually molested can be overpowering and horrifying as a parent. It's a difficult subject to broach, and many parents are confused about how to approach it. However, child sexual abuse can occur to any child, regardless of age, gender, ethnicity, or social background. It is not merely something that happens to "other" families or communities, it's a problem that impacts us all, and we all have a responsibility to keep our children safe.

This book, "Speaking Out: A Parent's Guide to Recognizing and Responding to the 7 Signs of Child Molestation," is intended to give parents the knowledge and resources they need to keep their children safe from sexual abuse. It is a detailed guide that covers the seven indicators of molestation, giving parents the knowledge, they need to detect these signs and take action to safeguard their children.

You will learn about the physical, behavioral, emotional, and cognitive indications of molestation in this book. You will comprehend when a child is sexually abused, as well as how it occurs and affects children. You'll also learn about common myths and misconceptions concerning child sexual abuse, as well as why it's critical to break the silence and speak up about this issue.

We will provide you with practical information and direction on how to respond if you fear your child has been sexually abused throughout this book. We will also provide advice on how to prevent child sexual abuse from occurring in the first place, as well as how to talk to your child about sexual abuse in an age-appropriate and powerful manner.

We recognize that this is a tough and delicate subject, and we want to assure you that we have addressed it with care and tenderness. Our mission is to offer you reliable, evidence-based information to assist you in keeping your child safe and healthy. We believe that this book will be a great resource for parents everywhere, raising awareness about the issue of child sexual abuse and encouraging more people to speak up and take action to safeguard children.

How to Use This Manual

This resource is designed to give parents the knowledge and tools they need to recognize and respond to indicators of child abuse. To make the most of this guide, follow these steps:

Read this book

Begin by reading this book from beginning to end. This course will teach you how to recognize the indications of molestation, how to respond if you fear your child has been molested, and how to prevent child sexual abuse.

Pay attention to the indicators

Be on the lookout for signs of molestation in your child. Physical, behavioral, emotional, cognitive, disclosure, grooming practices, and inappropriate language are all examples.

Talk to your youngster

Talk to your youngster in an open and honest manner concerning sexual abuse. Teach kids about proper boundaries and urge them to speak out if anyone bothers them or violates their boundaries.

Take urgent action

If you fear your child has been assaulted. This can include reporting the abuse to the relevant authorities, seeking medical assistance, and ensuring that your child receives the necessary support to heal.

Prevent child sexual abuse

Take action to avoid child sexual abuse in the first place. Teaching your child about bodily safety, monitoring their online activity, and being aware of the indications of grooming behavior are all examples of this.

Obtain assistance

If you require assistance or support, contact a certified professional who specializes in addressing child sexual assault. They may be able to help you negotiate this challenging problem, but you will need direction and assistance.

Remember that detecting the indicators of molestation is just the beginning. It is critical to act to protect your child and prevent further harm. By following this guidance, you will be better ready to recognize and respond to indicators of molestation, so protect your child from sexual abuse.

Chapter One

What Exactly Is Child Sex Abuse?

Child sexual abuse is a type of child maltreatment in which an adult or another kid who is much older or in a position of authority or control over the child engages in sexual behavior with the child. Physical contact such as fondling or penetration, non-contact abuse such as exposure to pornography or sexual discourse, and exploitation such as prostitution or trafficking are all examples of abuse. Child sexual abuse is a terrible and painful event for children, with long-term physical, emotional, and psychological consequences.

There are numerous definitions of child sexual abuse, but they all have some things in common. The World Health Organization (WHO) defines child sexual abuse as "the participation of a child in sexual activity that he or she does not fully comprehend, and is unable to give informed consent to, for which the child is not developmentally prepared and

cannot consent, or that violates the laws or social taboos of society"
(WHO, 2016).

Child sexual abuse can happen everywhere, including the home, school, religious organizations, and other communal contexts. It can be committed by someone the child knows and trusts, such as a family member, teacher, coach, or religious leader, or it might be committed by a stranger. In many circumstances, the abuser may employ grooming strategies to acquire the trust of the child and their family, making it more difficult for the youngster to disclose the abuse.

Child sexual abuse is a breach of a child's basic human rights and is a serious felony in many nations. In the United States, for example, all 50 states have laws that make child sexual abuse a crime, with punishments ranging from fines to prison time. Despite these regulations, child sexual abuse is a widespread problem, with millions of children worldwide being abused each year.

Child sexual abuse can have terrible and long-term consequences. Sexually abused children may have a variety of physical, emotional, and psychological symptoms, such as anxiety, sadness, PTSD, sleep difficulties, eating disorders, and self-harm. They may also struggle with relationships, trust, and intimacy, as well as building healthy ties with others. Furthermore, child sexual abuse, STIs, pregnancy, and physical injury are all bodily effects.

It is critical to highlight that child sexual abuse is never the child's responsibility. No kid should ever be blamed or shamed for their maltreatment, and parents and caregivers must create a safe and supportive environment for them to heal. Seeking professional assistance from a trained therapist or counselor who specializes in treating child sexual abuse can be a critical step in the healing process.

Child sexual abuse prevention is critical to safeguarding children from this heinous type of maltreatment. Teaching children about body safety and acceptable limits, monitoring their online activity, and being aware of the indications of grooming behavior are all examples of this. Additionally, it is critical to develop a society that does not tolerate child sexual abuse and to hold abusers accountable for their crimes. We can assist ensure that all children have the opportunity to grow and prosper in safety and security by working together to prevent child sexual abuse.

Myths And Misconceptions

There are many myths and misconceptions about child sexual abuse that can make it difficult for people to recognize and respond to this form of maltreatment. Some of the most common myths and misconceptions about child sexual abuse include:

Myth: Child sexual abuse only happens to girls.

Reality: Boys can also be victims of child sexual abuse. Studies have shown that boys make up a significant proportion of child sexual abuse victims.

Myth: Child sexual abuse occurs only in low-income families or in families with a history of abuse.

Reality: Regardless of social background, race, or ethnicity, child sexual abuse can occur in any family.

Myth: Child sexual abuse is always aggressive and physical.

Reality: Grooming strategies are used in many cases of child sexual abuse, in which the abuser earns the child's trust and manipulates them into engaging in sexual activities. This can involve emotional manipulation, gifts, special attention, or threats.

Myth: Sexually abused children will always inform someone.

Reality: Many sexually abused children do not report their abusers, either because they are terrified of the abuser, do not understand what has occurred to them, or are humiliated or embarrassed.

Myth: Child sexual abuse only occurs in very young children.

Reality: Child sexual abuse can happen to children of all ages, including teenagers. Adolescents are more likely to be sexually abused by their peers.

Myth: Only strangers sexually abuse children.

Reality: Many cases of child sexual abuse involve someone the child knows and trusts, such as a family member, teacher, coach, or religious leader.

Myth: If a child is sexually abused, they will always show physical signs of abuse.

Reality: Many children who are sexually assaulted do not show visible symptoms of abuse. Most cases of child sexual abuse do not involve physical contact.

Myth: Sexually abused children will grow up to be sexual predators.

Reality: There is no evidence to support this myth. In truth, many children sexual abuse survivors go on to live healthy and productive lives.

It's important to recognize and address these myths and misconceptions to better understand and respond to child sexual abuse. By debunking these stereotypes, we may contribute to the development of a society in which child sexual abuse is not allowed and victims are supported and empowered to heal.

The Consequences of Child Sexual Abuse

Child sexual abuse has terrible and long-term consequences for children. The impact of sexual abuse varies based on aspects such as the degree and duration of the abuse, the age of the kid, and the child's relationship with the abuser.

The following are some of the most common effects of sexual abuse on children:

Trauma, both psychological and emotional: Sexual abuse can result in long-term psychological and emotional distress. Sexually abused children may suffer from despair, anxiety, post-traumatic stress disorder (PTSD), and other mental health concerns. They may also experience feelings of humiliation, remorse, or low self-esteem.

Physical symptoms: Sexually abused children may have a variety of physical symptoms, including discomfort, headaches, and stomachaches. They may also experience sleep problems, eating disorders, and other physical health problems.

Behavioral issues: Children who have been sexually abused may exhibit a variety of behavioral issues, such as anger, withdrawal, and acting out. In addition, they may engage in dangerous activities such as substance addiction, self-harm, and sexual promiscuity.

Relationship issues: Sexual abuse can have a substantial impact on a child's capacity to build relationships. Children who have been sexually assaulted may have trust issues and find it difficult to build intimate relationships with others.

Sexual dysfunction: can also affect a child's sexual development and functioning. Children who have been sexually assaulted may struggle with sexual intimacy and develop sexual dysfunction later in life.

Impaired Development: Sexual abuse can impair a child's normal development and result in developmental problems. Sexually abused children may suffer from academic achievement, social skills, and other developmental milestones.

Increased risk of future victimization: Children who have been sexually abused may be more vulnerable to future victimization because they struggle with setting boundaries and detecting abusive conduct.

It is vital to emphasize that the consequences of sexual assault do not stop with the individual child who was abused. Sexual assault can also hurt families and communities, contributing to intergenerational cycles of abuse and trauma. We must take actions to prevent child sexual abuse while also assisting and empowering victims to heal and recover from the effects of this heinous kind of maltreatment.

Chapter Two

7 Signs of Child Abuse

Child molestation is a severe kind of child sexual abuse that can have far-reaching consequences for the victim. Recognizing the indicators of child molestation is critical for protecting children from future trauma and providing them with the healing help they require.

Here are seven indicators that a child has been abused:

1) Disclosure

Children who have been abused may disclose what happened to a trusted adult in a variety of ways, such as sketching drawings of the abuse or acting out the abuse during play.

2) Grooming Activities

These are acts used by abusers to acquire a child's trust and create a sense of familiarity and comfort. Giving gifts, paying extra attention, and spending alone time with the youngster are all examples of grooming activities.

3) Improper Use of Language

Using sexually explicit language, making improper sexual comments or jokes, or discussing sexual matters in front of or with minors are all examples of inappropriate language.

4) Physical Indicators

Physical indications of child molestation can be among the most evident indicators that a child has been sexually assaulted. It should be noted, however, that not all incidents of child molestation involve physical contact, and physical indications are not always present.

Here are some physical symptoms that indicate that a child has been abused:

- *Bruising, swelling, or bleeding in the genital area may indicate forced or traumatic sexual contact*.

- *Pain or discomfort in the genital area:* As a result of the abuse, children who have been abused may have pain or discomfort in the genital area.

- *Infection or genital discharge:* Sexual contact can result in genital infections or discharge.

- ***Children that have difficulty walking or sitting***: Because of the pain or discomfort caused by the assault, victims may have trouble walking or sitting.

- ***Underwear that is torn, discolored, or bloodied***: This could be a symptom of forced or violent sexual intercourse.

- ***Pregnancy or sexually transmitted illnesses***: Sexual abuse can result in pregnancy or sexually transmitted infections in extreme circumstances.

It is vital to recognize that physical symptoms alone do not prove that a child has been abused. Non-sexual causes may exist for some bodily symptoms, such as illnesses or traumas. If a child exhibits physical signs associated with sexual abuse, seek medical attention and report your concerns to the relevant authorities, such as child protective services or law enforcement.

In some circumstances, outward signs of child molestation may or may not be obvious or immediately apparent. Other indicators of child molestation include ***behavioral changes***, ***sexualized conduct***, ***and fear of a specific person or location***. If you feel a child has been abused, you should take their complaints seriously and seek expert treatment.

5) Behavioral Indicators

Some of the most essential evidence that a child has been sexually assaulted are behavioral signs of molestation. These cues may be less evident than physical indicators, but they can be just as dangerous. Here are some behavioral indicators of frequent molestation:

Changes in behavior: Children who have been abused may demonstrate behavioral changes such as withdrawal, anxiety, or depression. They may become angry or moody, and they may have problems sleeping or eating.

Sexualized conduct in children: Children who have been abused may demonstrate sexualized actions that are inappropriate for their age. For example, they may participate in sexual conduct with other children, become extremely interested in sex, or inappropriately touch themselves. Sexualized conduct is a common behavioral manifestation of child molestation and is especially problematic when displayed by young children. Sexualized conduct is defined as sexual behavior that exceeds what is developmentally suitable for a child's age. Here are some examples of sexualized conduct in children:

- *Playing "doctor" or other sexually explicit games with other children*: Children who have been abused may engage in sexual activity with other children, such as playing "doctor" or other sexually explicit games.

- *Inappropriate touching*: Molested children may inappropriately touch themselves or others, such as caressing their genitals in public or touching another person's genitals without consent.

- *Exhibitionism*: Children who have been sexually abused may indulge in exhibitionism, such as exposing their genitals in public or engaging in sexual actions in front of others.

- *Sexualized language*: Children who have been abused may use sexualized vocabulary that is inappropriate for their age, such as discussing sexual acts or using sexually explicit phrases.

- *Masturbation*: Children who have been abused may indulge in masturbation at an early age or in an inappropriate manner.

- *Obsessive interest in sexual content*: Children who have been abused may become too curious about sex and develop a strong interest in sexual content such as pornography or sexual literature.

It is crucial to highlight that sexualized conduct does not always imply that a kid has been abused, and not all children who exhibit sexualized behavior have been abused. Sexualized conduct that is not developmentally appropriate, on the other hand, can be a warning sign that a child has been exposed to sexual information or sexual activity that is beyond their comprehension or comfort level.

If you witness a child engaging in sexualized conduct, you should approach the problem with caution and seek expert assistance. A qualified counselor or therapist can assist the youngster in understanding their behavior and developing suitable ways of expressing themselves. To maintain the child's safety and well-being, any suspicions of sexual abuse should be reported to the relevant authorities, such as child protective services or police enforcement.

Fear and Avoidance: Children who have been abused may be afraid of a specific person or place. They may develop scared of being alone with a specific individual, or they may avoid traveling to a specific location where the abuse occurred. Another prominent behavioral indication of child molestation is the avoidance of certain people or situations. Avoiding family members, friends, or other trustworthy adults who were involved in the abuse or who may remind the child of the abuse is one example.

A youngster who has been molested by their uncle, for example, may avoid family gatherings or become anxious when their uncle is around. Similarly, a child who has been molested in a specific location, such as a specific room in their home or a park, may avoid that spot or become disturbed when they visit it.

Avoiding particular persons or locations might be a protective technique for the youngster, who may feel frightened or vulnerable in these circumstances. It can, however, make it difficult for the child to engage in usual activities and can have an effect on their interactions with others.

It is critical to handle a child's avoidance behavior with tact and to attempt to comprehend their concerns. It's also critical to offer a safe and supportive atmosphere for the youngster, as well as work with them to develop coping methods to deal with their worry and dread. A qualified counselor or therapist can assist the youngster in processing their emotions and developing techniques for dealing with abuse-related issues.

If a child's avoidance behavior is due to ongoing abuse or a possible risk, any concerns should be reported to the relevant authorities to ensure the child's safety and well-being, such as child protective services or police enforcement.

Secretive: Children who have been sexually abused may become secretive about their activities and locations. They may be hesitant to share their day or experiences with others, or they may become evasive when questioned.

Alterations in Dietary Habits:

Changes in eating patterns can also be an indication of child molestation. Molested children may endure a variety of emotional and psychological symptoms, including anxiety, despair, and post-traumatic stress disorder (PTSD). These reactions can have a variety of effects on a child's appetite and eating habits.

One common traumatic response is a loss of interest in food or a drop in appetite. Children may feel sick, have stomach pains, or have trouble swallowing food. They may also feel guilty or ashamed, which may result in a loss of appetite or avoidance of meals. As a result, some children may restrict their food consumption as a way of self-punishment or to reclaim control over their bodies.

On the other side, some children may overeat in order to cope with the mental discomfort of being abused. They may turn to food for solace, leading to emotional eating or binge eating. This might result in weight gain, which can exacerbate the child's emotional anguish and bad attitudes about their body.

Changes in eating patterns can be a crucial indicator when a youngster is suffering emotional discomfort or trauma. If you observe a child's eating habits changing, it's crucial to approach the problem sensitively and try to understand their concerns. Encouraging the youngster to express their feelings and emotions may be beneficial and assist them in processing their trauma and developing appropriate coping strategies. A qualified counselor or therapist can also assist the youngster in working through emotional issues and developing techniques for controlling their eating habits.

If a child's eating habits alter as a result of continuous abuse or possible danger, it's critical to notify the relevant authorities, such as child protective services or law enforcement, to safeguard the child's safety and well-being.

6) Emotional Indications

Emotional signs of molestation might be difficult to detect, yet they are vital markers that a child has been sexually abused. Emotional indicators may include:

Fear and Phobias: Molested children may acquire illogical fears or phobias. They may become afraid of certain people or circumstances, leading to avoidance behavior. A child, for example, may develop a fear of being alone or in the dark.

Anger and hostility: Molested children may have tremendous feelings of rage or hostility. They may lash out at others, become easily upset or impatient, and struggle with emotional control.

Self-harm: Molested children may engage in self-harm activities such as slashing or burning themselves. This could be a technique for them to cope with the emotional agony they're going through.

Regression: Children who have been abused may exhibit behaviors more typical of younger children. A youngster who has been potty-trained, for example, may begin wetting the bed, or a child who has been speaking in entire phrases may begin mumbling.

Sleep Disturbances: Molested children may have sleep disturbances such as nightmares, night terrors, or difficulties sleeping or staying asleep.

Emotional Instability

Children who have been abused may develop emotional instability, such as mood swings or emotional outbursts.

It is critical to respond sensitively to emotional indications and to offer a safe and supportive environment for the youngster to process their emotions. Counseling or therapy can be beneficial for children who have undergone sexual abuse since it can offer them support, strategies to cope with their emotions, and good coping mechanisms. To preserve the child's safety and well-being, any concerns should be reported to the relevant authorities, such as child protective services or law enforcement.

Depression and Anxiety

Molested children may feel depressed or have anxiety. They may be depressed or pessimistic, and they may experience difficulties sleeping or concentrating. They could also feel useless, guilty, or ashamed. Anxiety and despair can have a significant impact.

It is critical to acknowledge that anxiety and sadness are normal reactions to trauma and that children who have been sexually abused may require professional assistance to cope with these emotions. Counseling or therapy can be beneficial for children who have been sexually abused because it can teach them how to cope with their feelings and establish appropriate coping mechanisms.

How To Care for A Child Who Has Anxiety and Depression as A Result Of Childhood Sexual Abuse

Caring for a child who suffers from anxiety and depression as a result of child molestation can be difficult and demanding, but it is critical that they receive the assistance and care they require to cope with their feelings and heal from their trauma. Here are some things you may do to help a youngster who is anxious or depressed:

Seek Professional Assistance

Seeking professional help is the first step in caring for a child who has anxiety and depression as a result of child molestation. A therapist or counselor who works with children who have been sexually abused can provide the child with the tools and support they need to cope with their feelings and heal from their trauma.

Promote Open Communication

Open communication with the child is critical to their recovery process. Inform them that they can contact you and that you are there to listen and support them while they express their experiences and emotions to you. Avoid judging or criticizing their emotions, and assure them that it is normal to feel sad or furious.

Make Your Workplace Safe and Comfortable

Providing a safe and supportive atmosphere for a child's healing is critical. Make sure the youngster feels at ease and safe in their surroundings, and avoid exposing them to circumstances or individuals who may cause anxiety or depression. Providing them with a feeling of routine and stability can also help alleviate their anxiety and despair.

Promote Self-Care

Encourage the youngster to participate in self-care activities to help them cope with their anxiety and despair. Exercise, meditation, and artistic endeavors can all reduce stress and enhance a sense of well-being. Encourage them to participate in activities they enjoy, and try to schedule time for them together.

Provide Emotional Support

Emotional support is essential for a child's healing process. Make it clear to them that they are not to blame for the abuse and that they are still deserving of love and respect. Offer them words of support and affirmation, and let them know you are always there for them.

Caring for a child who has anxiety and depression as a result of child molestation can be difficult, but children can heal and overcome their trauma with the correct support and care, seeking professional assistance, fostering open communication, and establishing a secure environment Providing a supportive environment, fostering self-care, and providing emotional support are all critical stages in caring for a child who has been sexually abused.

Self-Esteem Issues

Children who have been abused may have low self-esteem. They may believe they are at fault for the abuse or that they are damaged or imperfect in some way. This might result in feelings of shame and isolation, and it can have an influence on the child's capacity to build healthy relationships with others.

It is critical to convince children who have been abused that they are not to blame for the abuse and that they are still worthy of love and respect. Encourage them to participate in activities that they enjoy and that increase their confidence.

Caring for a child who has poor self-esteem as a result of molestation can be difficult, but it is critical that they receive the support and care they require to heal from their trauma and build their self-confidence. Here are some things you can do to help a child who has poor self-esteem:

Promote Positive Self-Talk

Positive self-talk is vital for increasing a child's self-esteem. Assist the youngster in identifying their positive characteristics and encouraging them to focus on their strengths rather than their flaws. Instead of criticizing or dismissing the child, offer words of support and affirmation.

Make Opportunities for Success Available

Providing the opportunity for the youngster to succeed can be beneficial in assisting in the development of their self-esteem. Encourage the child to participate in activities that he or she enjoys and is good at, and applaud their accomplishments, no matter how minor they may appear. This can help to increase their self-esteem and confidence.

Provide Emotional Support

Emotional support is essential for a child's healing process. Make it clear to them that they are not to blame for the abuse and that they are still deserving of love and respect. Offer them words of support and affirmation, and let them know you are always there for them.

Make Your Workplace Safe and Comfortable

Providing a safe and supportive atmosphere for a child's healing is critical. Make sure the child is at ease and safe in their surroundings, and keep them away from circumstances or individuals that may trigger their anxiety or despair. Providing them with a sense of routine and stability can also help alleviate their low self-esteem.

Seek Professional Assistance

Seeking expert help is critical for a child's healing. A therapist or counselor who specializes in working with children who have undergone sexual abuse can help the youngster cope with their feelings and enhance their self-esteem.

Caring for a child who has poor self-esteem as a result of molestation can be difficult, but children can heal and reclaim their feeling of self-worth with the correct support and care. Encouraging positive self-talk, providing opportunities for accomplishment, providing emotional support, and establishing a supportive environment, as well as seeking professional assistance, are all critical stages in caring for a child who has undergone sexual abuse and has poor self-esteem.

Mood Swings

Children who have been abused may have mood swings. They may become impatient or angry out of nowhere, or they may appear withdrawn and aloof. These mood fluctuations can be difficult to comprehend and might be perplexing for caregivers or loved ones.

Children who are experiencing mood swings should be approached with care and understanding. Allowing them to express their sensations and emotions can assist them in processing their trauma and developing appropriate coping skills.

Creating a safe and supportive workplace can also aid in mitigating the effects of changes in mood.

Anxiety and despair, low self-esteem, and mood swings are all emotional markers of molestation that can be difficult to detect but are key indicators that a child has been sexually abused. It is important to respond sensitively to these emotional cues and to create a safe and supportive environment for the youngster to process their emotions. Counseling or therapy can be beneficial for children who have been sexually abused because it can teach them how to cope with their feelings and establish appropriate coping mechanisms.

How To Love and Care for A Child That Suffers from Mood Swings Due to Molestation

Caring for a child that suffers from mood swings can be difficult, but it is critical to offer them love and care to help them cope with their feelings.

Here are some ideas for how to love and care for a child who has mood swings:

Validate Their Emotions
It is critical to validate the child's feelings and assure them that what they are feeling is valid and understandable with encouragement and support.

Make a Safe Zone

Providing a safe environment for the youngster is critical to their healing process. Maintain their comfort and security in their surroundings, and avoid exposing them to events or individuals that may provoke their mood swings. This can help them feel less anxious and more in control of their emotions.

Assist Them in Developing Coping Skills

Helping the youngster develop coping skills can help them manage their mood fluctuations. Teach them calming techniques like deep breathing or meditation, and encourage them to participate in physical activities like yoga or exercise. These abilities can assist individuals in managing their emotions and decreasing the frequency of their mood swings.

Promote Communication

Encouragement of the youngster to assist them in identifying and naming their feelings and providing words of encouragement. Encouraging the child to communicate their feelings is important for their healing process. Let them know that it's safe to express their emotions, and listen to them without judgment. Offer words of support and encouragement, and help them find healthy ways to express their emotions.

Seek Professional Help

Seeking professional help is essential for a child's healing process. A therapist or counselor who specializes in working with children who have experienced sexual abuse can provide the child with the tools and support they need to manage their emotions and cope with their mood swings.

Caring for a child with mood swings as a result of molestation requires patience, understanding, and empathy. Validating their feelings, creating a safe space, helping them develop coping skills, encouraging communication, and seeking professional help are all important steps in loving and caring for a child who has experienced sexual abuse and has mood swings. With the right support and care, children can heal and regain their sense of emotional stability.

Communication, as well as seeking professional help, are all critical elements in loving and caring for a child who has been sexually abused and suffers mood swings. Children can heal and restore emotional stability with the correct support and care.

7) Cognitive symptoms

Child molestation has been shown to have a negative impact on a child's cognitive functioning. The following are some of the most common cognitive indicators of molestation:

Concentration Difficulties

Children who have been molested may find it difficult to focus on tasks or activities. They may appear distracted or disengaged, and they may have difficulty following directions or completing assignments. This can have an impact on their academic achievement as well as their capacity to participate in daily activities.

Memory Issues

Children who have been abused may have trouble remembering facts, particularly details about the abuse. They may forget crucial dates, events, or facts pertaining to their everyday activities. This can have an impact on their capacity to absorb and remember new information, as well as their social relationships.

Perplexity and Disorientation

Children who have been molested may be confused or disoriented about what has occurred to them. They may be confused about their emotions and sentiments, and they may feel overwhelmed or helpless. This can have an impact on their capacity to make decisions and navigate their daily lives.

Flashbacks and Nightmares

Children who have been abused may suffer dreams and flashbacks relating to the trauma. They may have intrusive thoughts or memories during the day, or they may wake up in the middle of the night with vivid memories of the abuse. This can disrupt their sleeping cycles and cause anxiety and panic.

Self-Image Problems

Children who have been abused may acquire a bad self-image. They may feel humiliated, embarrassed, or guilty about what has happened to them They may blame themselves for what occurred to them. This can have an impact on their self-esteem and confidence, as well as their social interactions.

Trust Issues

Children who have been abused may have trouble trusting others. They may be cautious of strangers or people they do not know well, and they may struggle to build close relationships. This might have an impact on their social development and cause feelings of isolation or loneliness.

Numbness on the Emotional Level

Children who have been abused may become emotionally numb or alienated from their feelings. They may look apathetic or disinterested in situations or events, and they may struggle to convey their feelings. This can have an impact on their ability to build deep relationships and lead to feelings of loneliness or isolation.

It should be noted that not all children who have been abused will exhibit these cognitive indicators. Some children may exhibit no symptoms at all, while others may exhibit a variety of symptoms. It's critical to be aware of these warning signs and to seek professional help if you feel a child has been abused. A qualified expert can assist the youngster in managing emotions, developing coping skills, and working toward healing and recovery.

Chapter Three

What to Do If a Child Reports Abuse

It is critical to respond in a helpful and acceptable manner if a child admits that they have been assaulted. Here are some crucial actions to take:

Trust the Child

The first and most crucial step is to trust the child. Children who have been abused may feel humiliated, terrified, or bewildered, and may be reluctant to speak up. It is critical to affirm the child's emotions and reassure them that what occurred was not their fault.

Maintain Calm and Reassurance

It is critical to be calm and soothing when a youngster exposes abuse. Assure the youngster that they are safe and that you are there to help them. Avoid expressing your rage or dissatisfaction, as this can be harmful and make the child feel guilty or embarrassed.

Validate and Listen

It is critical to attentively listen to and validate the child's version of what occurred. Make it clear to the child that you believe them and that they did the right thing by speaking out. Asking leading questions or attempting to fill in details can jeopardize the child's narrative.

Please Report the Abuse.

It is critical that the abuse be reported to the relevant authorities, such as police enforcement or child protective services. This can assist in protecting the youngster and preventing additional abuse. Prepare to provide as much information as possible, such as the child's name, age, and any facts about the abuse.

Seek Professional Assistance

Children who have been molested may benefit from counseling or therapy as examples of professional assistance. A qualified expert can assist the youngster in managing emotions, developing coping skills, and working toward healing and recovery. Prepare to seek out community resources, such as a local advocacy center or mental health facility.

Maintain Your Privacy

It is critical to maintain confidentiality and protect the privacy of the child. Avoid discussing the abuse with anyone who isn't directly engaged, and doesn't share any specifics on social media or other public places. This can aid in the protection of the child's emotional well-being and the prevention of additional trauma.

Follow-up and Assistance

Following a child's disclosure of abuse, it is critical to follow up and give continuous support. Check-in with the youngster on a frequent basis and make yourself accessible to listen and provide emotional support. Continue to seek professional assistance if necessary, and to collaborate with the child's caretakers to build an ongoing care and support plan.

In summary, responding to a child who reveals abuse requires sensitivity, compassion, and appropriate action. You may assist protect the child, providing emotional support, and striving toward healing and recovery by taking these critical measures.

Preventive Strategies for Child Sexual Abuse

Preventing child sexual abuse is critical to safeguarding children's safety and well-being. Here are some prevention tips for child sexual abuse:

Children should be educated.

Teach youngsters about personal boundaries and how to say "no" when someone inappropriately touches them. Teach kids that it is alright to speak up if someone touches them in an unpleasant way.

Recognize the symptoms of child sexual abuse.

As described in previous chapters of this book, it is critical to detect the indicators of child sexual abuse in order to protect the child from further injury.

Create a secure environment.

Create a nurturing and safe environment for children. Encourage open conversation, pay attention to their worries, and validate their emotions.

Potential abusers should be screened.

Conduct extensive background checks and screening processes when hiring caregivers, instructors, or other individuals who will have contact with children.

Set firm boundaries.

Make obvious distinctions between youngsters and adults. Allow adults to be alone with children in private settings, for example.

Keep an eye out for online activities.

Keep an eye on your children's online behavior and be aware of the dangers of online predators.

Speak out!

Speak up if you feel a child is being mistreated and report it to the right authorities. Do not remain mute and expect someone else to take action.

Seek Assistance.

Seek professional treatment and support if you or someone you know has been a victim of child sexual abuse. It is critical in order to recover and go on, it is necessary to process the trauma and learn coping techniques.

We can help prevent child sexual abuse and protect children by putting these procedures in place.

- **Reporting Abuse to the Authorities**

Reporting child abuse to the authorities is a critical step in protecting children from further harm and holding abusers accountable for their actions. In this chapter, we will discuss the measures that should be taken to report abuse to the appropriate authorities.

Determine the Correct Authority

The first step in reporting abuse is to identify the appropriate authority. Depending on the circumstances, the following authorities may need to be contacted:

Law Enforcement

If the abuse is recent or ongoing, and there is a risk of immediate harm to the child, law enforcement should be contacted immediately. This could include municipal police or sheriff's departments, as well as state-level law enforcement agencies like the state police or highway patrol, Child Protective Services (CPS), should be called if the abuse has occurred in the past or is ongoing but there is no imminent risk of damage. CPS is in charge of investigating complaints of child abuse and safeguarding children's safety.

If the abuse occurs at school or is related to school activities, school officials such as teachers, counselors, or administrators should be alerted. They can assist in ensuring the protection of the child and may be compelled by law to report suspected abuse.

Medical Professionals: If the abuse has resulted in bodily harm or illness, doctors, nurses, or hospital staff should be alerted. They can give medical attention and document any signs of abuse.

It is critical to collect as much information as possible before writing a report. This could include:

I. *Name, age, and contact information for the child*

II. *The alleged abuser's name and contact information Specifics concerning the abuse, such as when it occurred, where it occurred, and what happened*

III. *Abuse-related bodily evidence, such as bruises or injuries*

IV. *Any witness statements or other evidence*

It is critical to be as clear and detailed as possible, as this will assist investigators and authorities in taking necessary action.

- **Create the Report**

Once the right authority has been recognized and information has been acquired, it's time to make the report. This may involve:

Using a hotline

Many states and municipalities establish hotlines where you can report suspected child abuse. These Hotlines are often staffed 24 hours a day, seven days a week, and can provide quick support and information.

Producing an online report

Online reporting of suspected child abuse is permitted in several states and municipalities. This can be a quick and private way to submit a report.

Contacting police enforcement or CPS directly: It may be necessary to call law enforcement or CPS directly in some circumstances. This may entail contacting your local police department's non-emergency number or your state's CPS agency.

When writing a report, it is critical to provide as much information as possible while remaining as clear and succinct as feasible. Stick to the facts and avoid forming assumptions or drawing inferences.

- **Following Up**

Following the completion of a report, it is critical to follow up with the right authorities to guarantee that proper action is taken. This could include:

- If requested, providing further information or evidence inquiring about the child's well-being

- Taking part in any investigation or legal proceedings
- It is critical to maintain the investigation's confidentially and avoid discussing the matter with anybody who is not immediately engaged.

It can be a tough and painful procedure to report suspected child abuse, but it is critical for protecting children and bringing perpetrators accountable. You can assist ensure that proper action is taken and that children are kept safe by following these steps.

Support and More Information Resources

If you or someone you know is experiencing or has been affected by child sexual abuse, it is critical that you seek support and assistance. Here are some places for additional help and information:

- **National Sexual Assault Hotline**: The National Sexual Assault Hotline helps survivors of sexual assault, especially child sexual abuse, with confidential assistance and services. The hotline is available 24 hours a day, seven days a week at 1-800-656-4673.

- **Child help National Child Abuse Hotline**: The Child help National Child Abuse Hotline provides crisis assistance, information, and referrals to children and families who have been abused, especially sexually abused children. The hotline can be called 24 hours a day, seven days a week, at 1-800-422-4453.

- Darkness to Light is a non-profit organization dedicated to the abolition of child sexual abuse. They provide people with information, training, and support in order for them to prevent, recognize, and respond responsibly to child sexual abuse. More information can be found at www.d2l.org.

- National Children's Alliance: The National Children's Alliance is a non-profit organization that supports the nationwide network of Children's Advocacy Centers (CACs). CACs offer comprehensive treatment to children and families who have experienced child abuse, including sexual assault. More information can be found at www.nationalchildrensalliance.org.

- Stop It Now! is a non-profit organization dedicated to preventing child sexual abuse by providing people and families with resources, support, and education. More information can be found at www.stopitnow.org.

- RAINN (Rape, Abuse, and Incest National Network): RAINN (Rape, Abuse, and Incest National Network) is the nation's largest anti-sexual violence group. They offer assistance as well as resources for survivors of sexual assault, especially child sexual abuse.

Remember, you are not alone and there is aid available. It is crucial to seek support and tools to help you or someone you love heal and recover from the trauma of child sexual abuse.

Conclusion

The indicators of child molestation might be subtle and difficult to detect, but it is critical to be watchful and aware in order to protect children from harm. Child sexual abuse can have long-term and catastrophic consequences for a child's physical, emotional, and cognitive well-being. It is our job as a society to prevent child sexual abuse and to support those who have been touched by it.

We may try to make the world a safer place for children through education, communication, and prevention efforts. It is critical to teach youngsters about personal boundaries and how to speak up if they feel unsafe or uncomfortable. We must also know the indications of child sexual abuse and respond if we feel a child is being abused.

It is critical to provide a safe environment for children, which involves screening potential abusers, setting clear boundaries, and monitoring internet activities. It is also critical to speak up and report any suspected abuse to the proper authorities.

When a child confesses abuse, it is critical to listen to and believe them, as well as to provide support and care and report the abuse to authorities. We must not criticize or shame the child, but rather provide a safe and supportive atmosphere in which they can heal and recover.

As a society, we must also endeavor to dispel myths and prejudices about child sexual abuse, as well as promote open communication and support culture for those impacted.

Finally, acknowledging and responding to indicators of child molestation is an important step toward safeguarding children from harm and building a better society for all. We can prevent child sexual abuse and support those who have been touched by it by working together, allowing them to heal and thrive.